I0462394

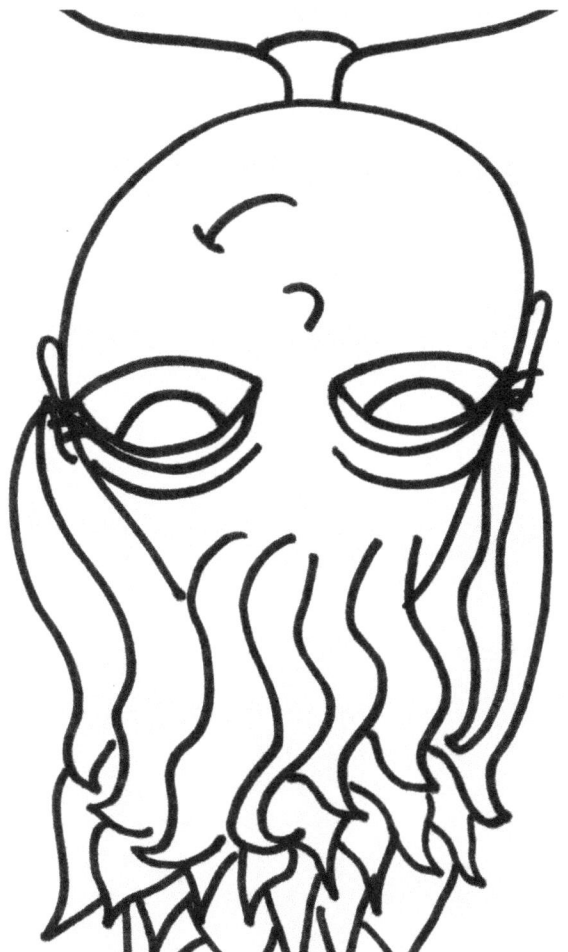

ISBN-13: 978-1530897254

ISBN-10: 1530897254

Welcome to My Mantra Colouring Book: A Yogini's Journey! Thank you so much for your purchase.

As a Yoga and Meditation teacher I've found many to love the exploration of mantra. Chanting the sacred sounds, be it aloud or silently, can create great change. The practice also invites a greater sense of peace and wellbeing in our daily lives.

Whether you decide to set a 40 day intention using these mantras or you simply love their essence and meanings I hope you enjoy it. Go grab your markers, pens, pencil crayons or paints and your creative juices!

You could use this book to write the mantras 108x in the backgrounds on the images that have room to do so. Some, like the Gayatri Mantra, are too large although most have ample room available for you. Read them daily and watch the changes unfold in your life! You could put your creations into a frame on your altar and use the additional energies to remind you of the space within that is sacred. Light a candle or burn some incense and create!

I would suggest placing a piece of paper (you could also choose waxed paper) behind the pictures particularly if you are choosing wet mediums to prevent any bleed-through. The pictures have a page between them to help with this additionally. However if you, like me, enjoy using acrylics or watercolour you may need the additional support for the page.

You'll find lots of areas in the pictures to add additional creations; as I mentioned you could write the mantras in the background. Or why not turn it into a journal by writing about your day in the blank areas, play with some interesting fonts or add your favourite affirmations? So many choices here and the opportunity to expand the pictures to your perfect design.

Not sure of the meaning or how to pronounce the mantras shown? A fast internet search can help you along your journey. Keep in mind it is the intention behind your chanting that will help the most.

You are the artist here so whatever you create will be perfect!

Happy colouring & chanting.

Wishing you many continued blessings.

Namaste,

Tammy

Om Mani Padme Hum

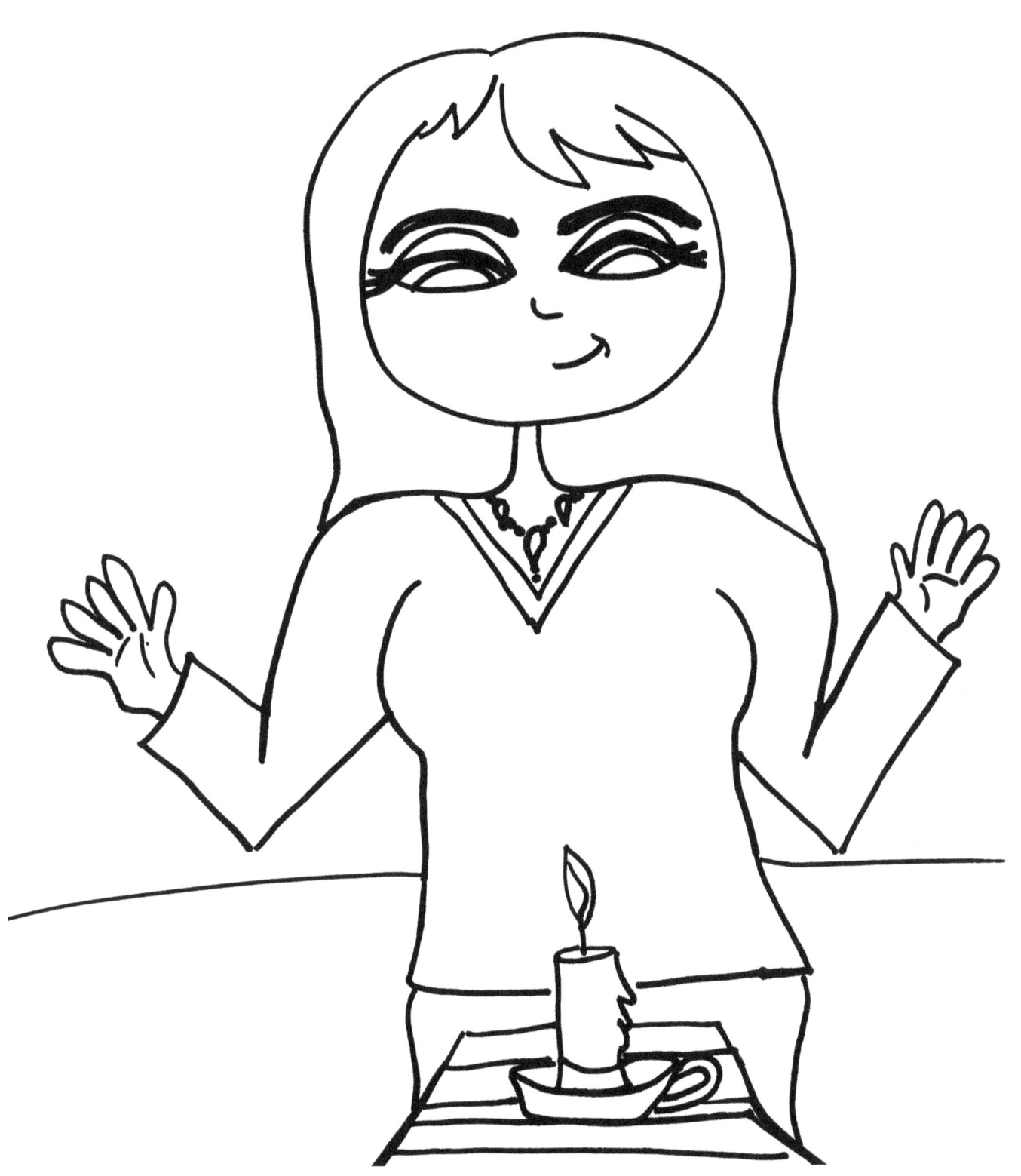

Om Namah Shivaya

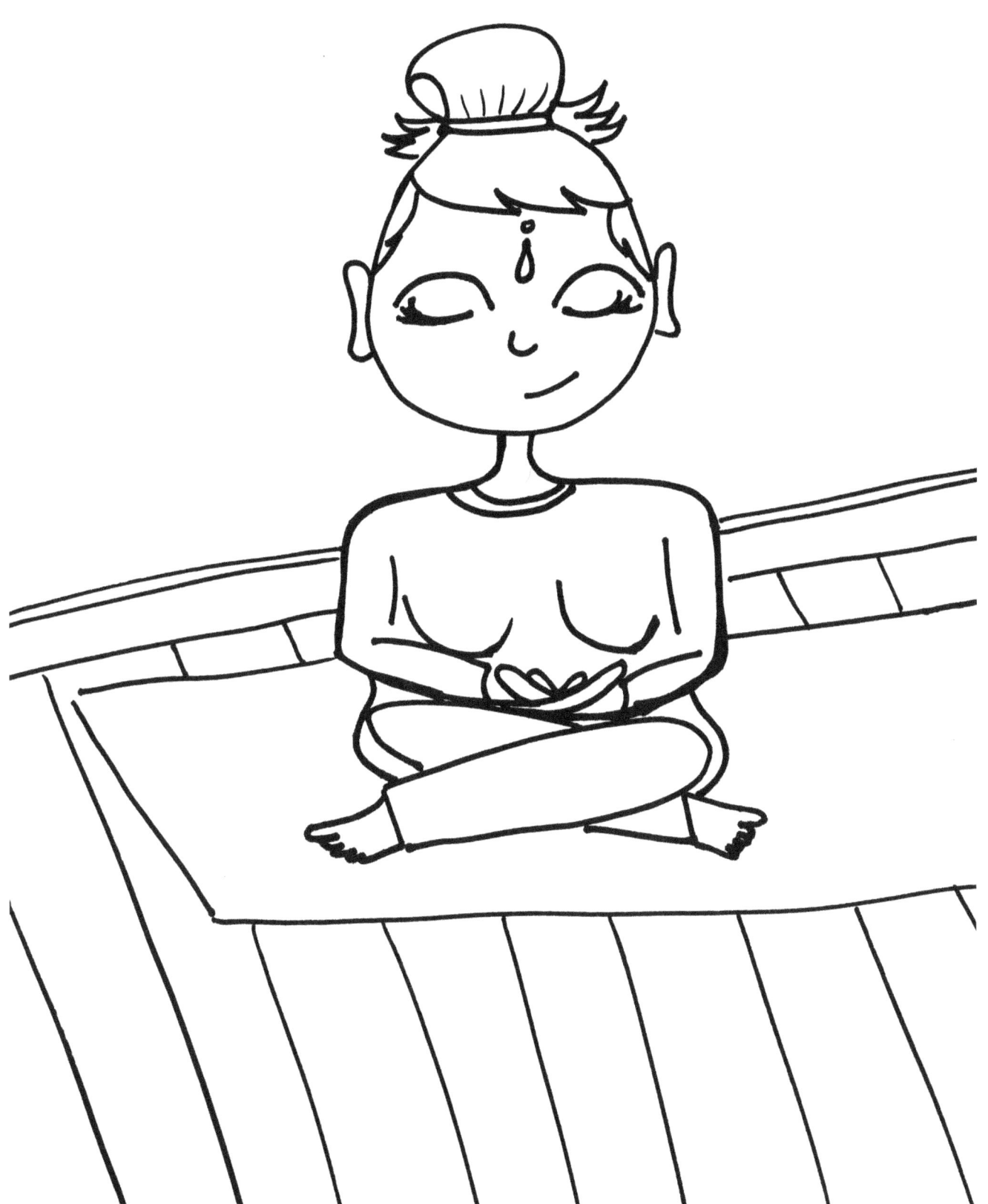

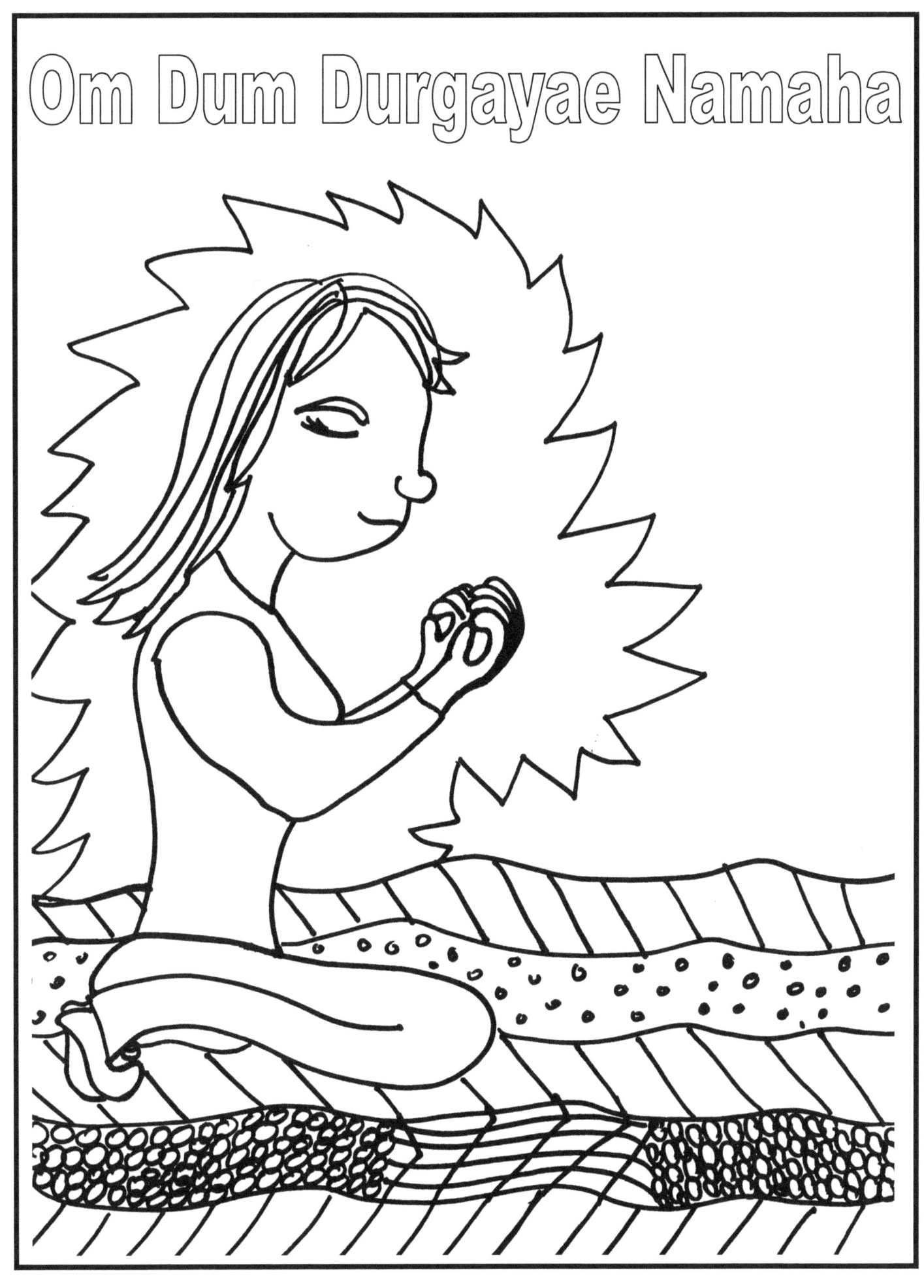

Om Shreem Maha Lakshmiyei Swaha

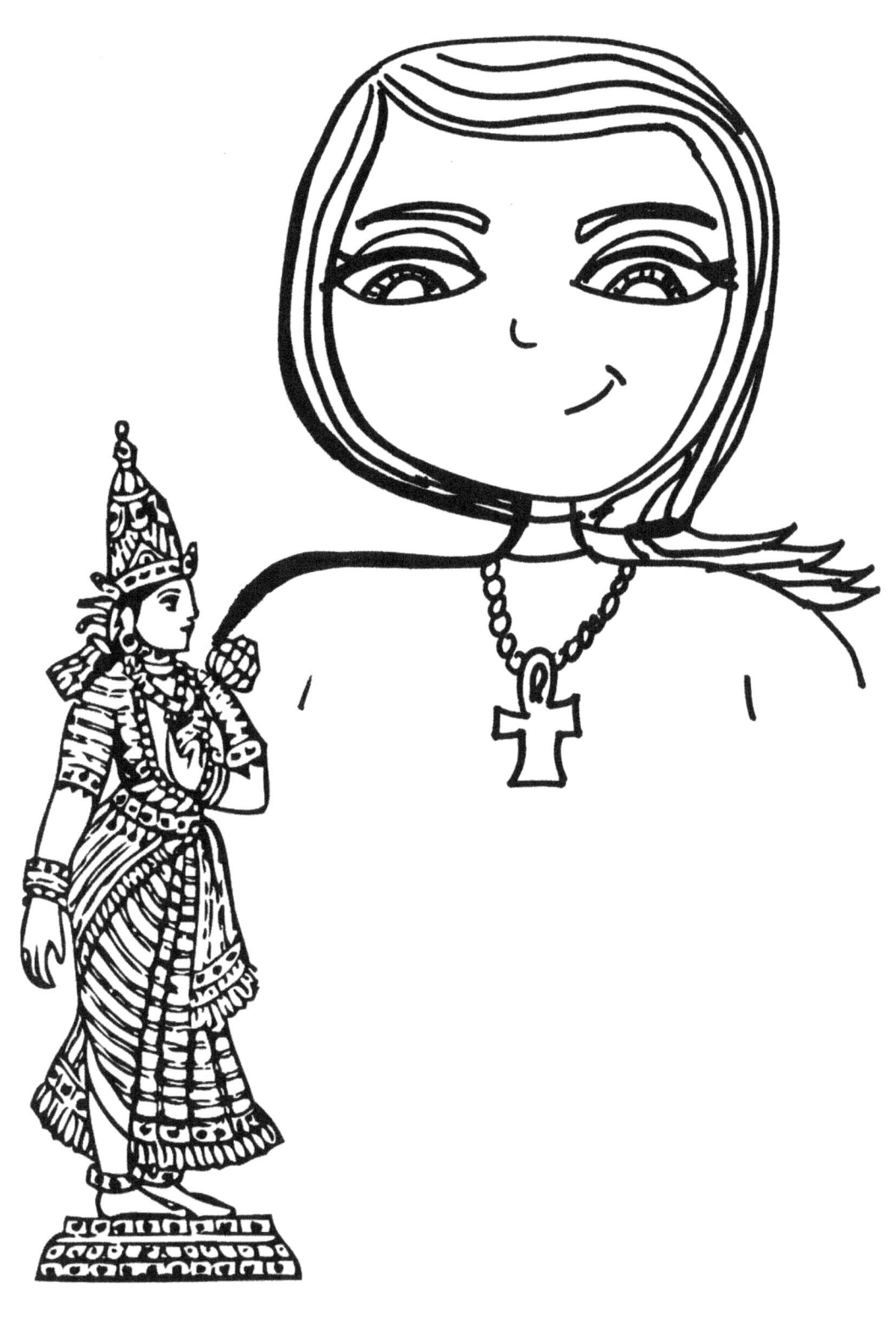

Om Gum Ganapatayae Namaha

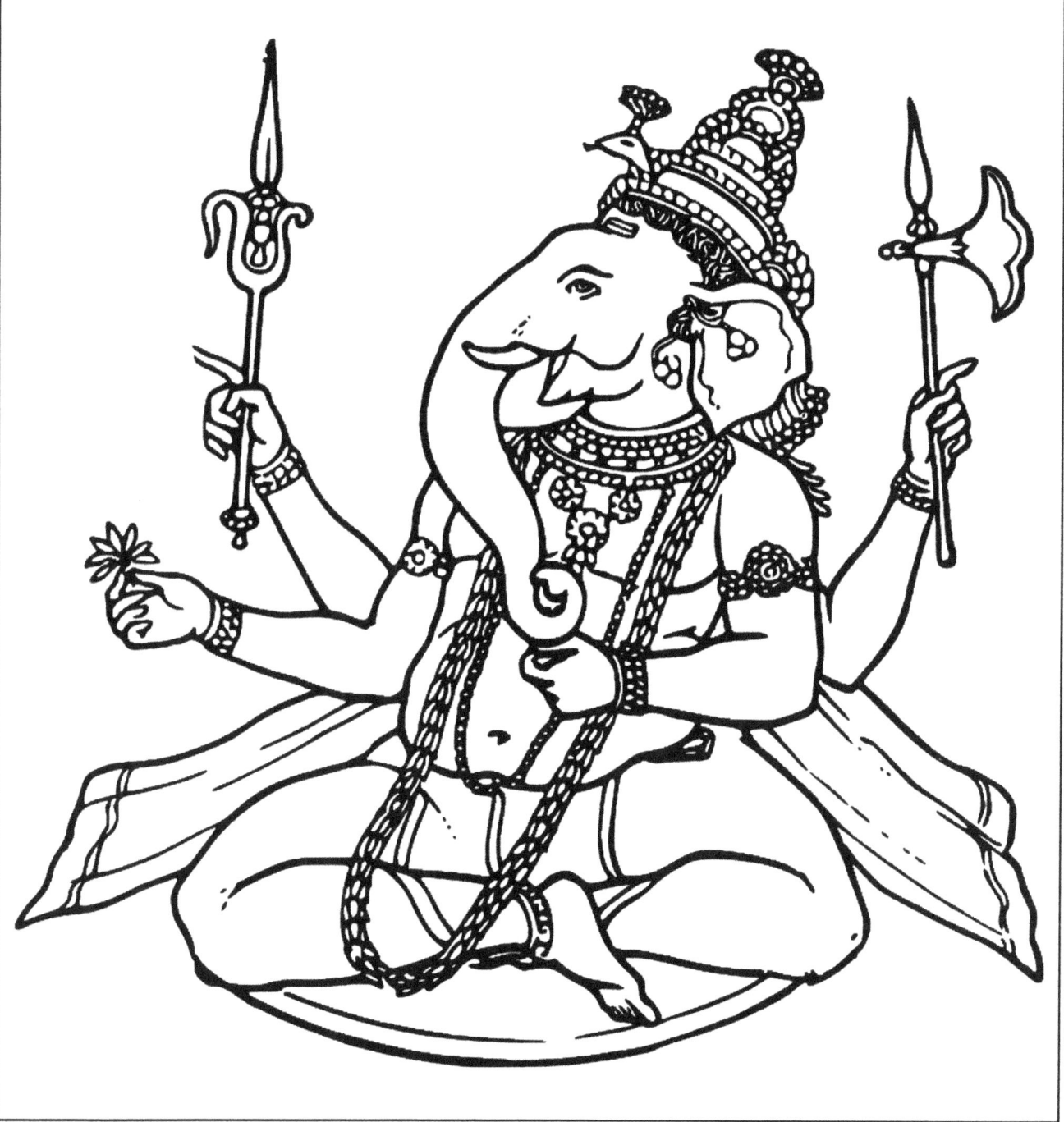

Ahum Brayhma

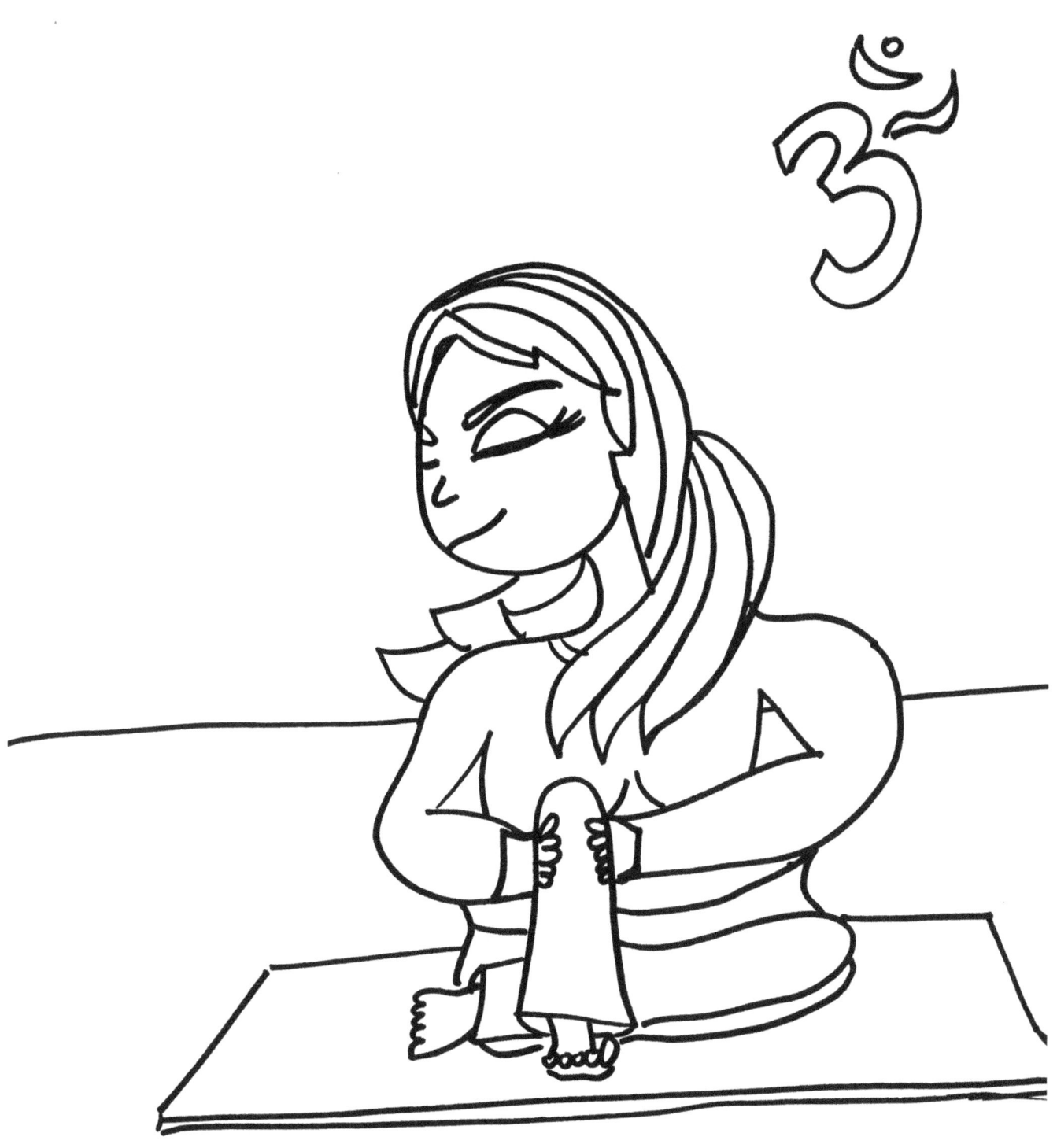

Gayatri Mantra
Om Bhur Bhuvas svaha
Thath savithur varaynyam
Bhargo dheyvasya dhimahih
dhyoyonah pratchodhay-yath

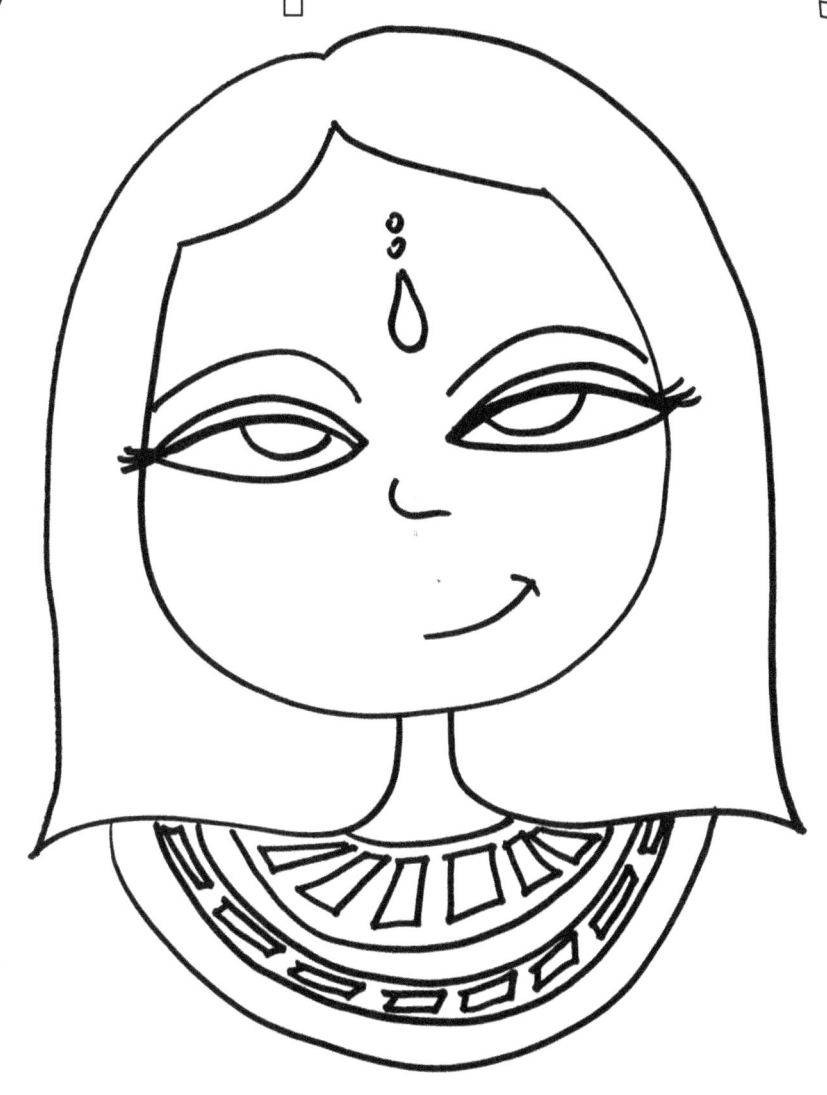

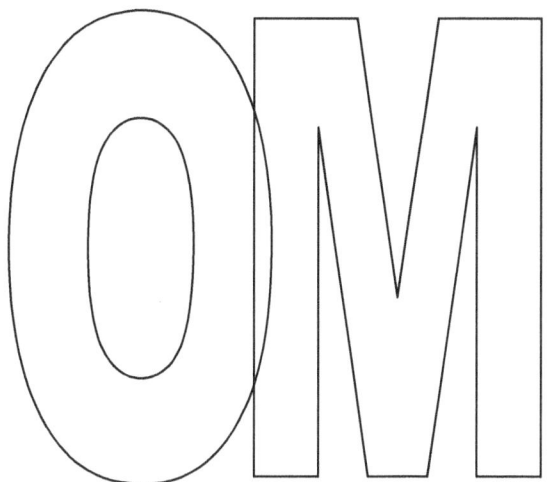

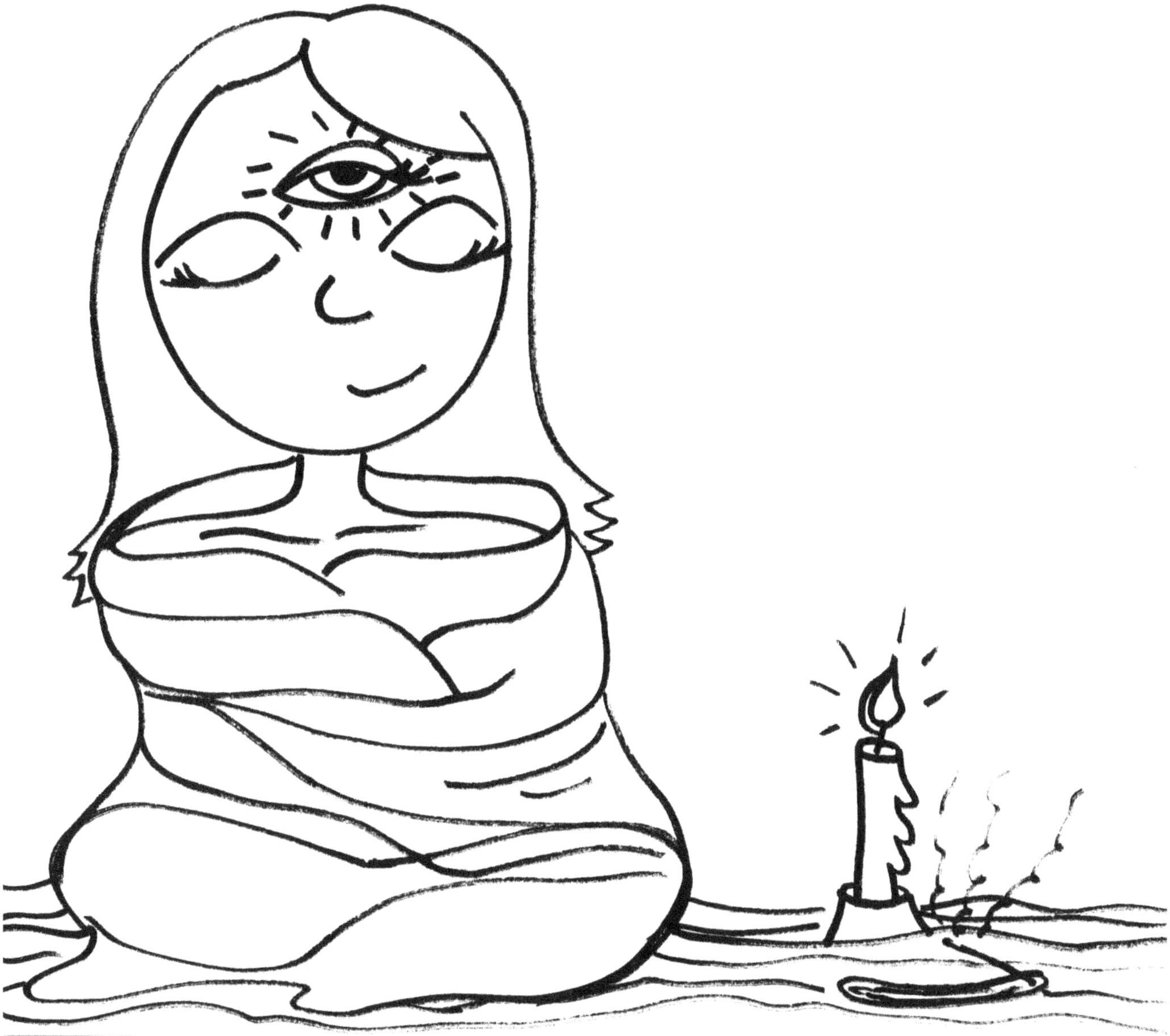

Ram

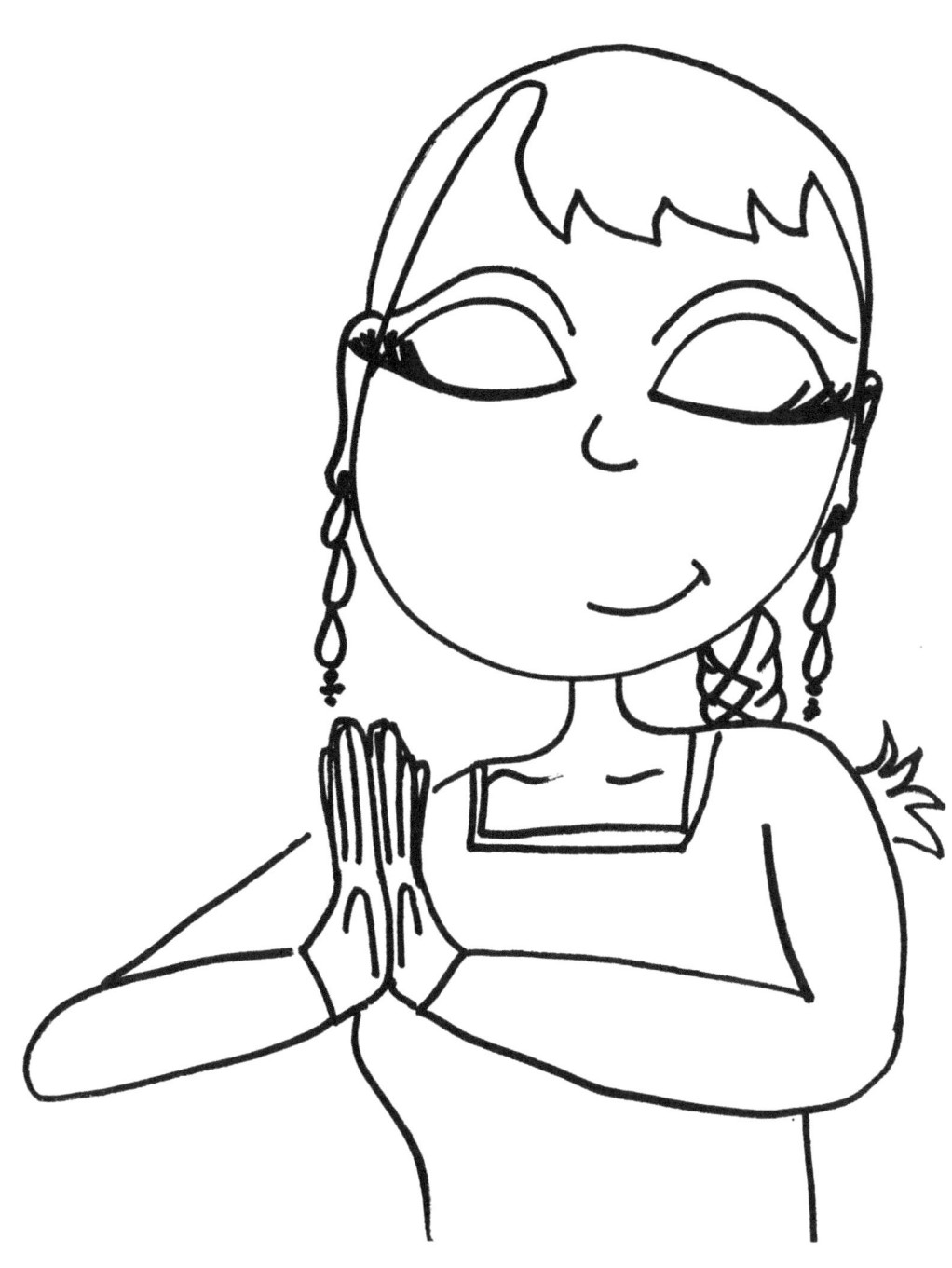

Lokah Samastah
Sukhino Bhavantu

Om Namo Guru Dav Namo

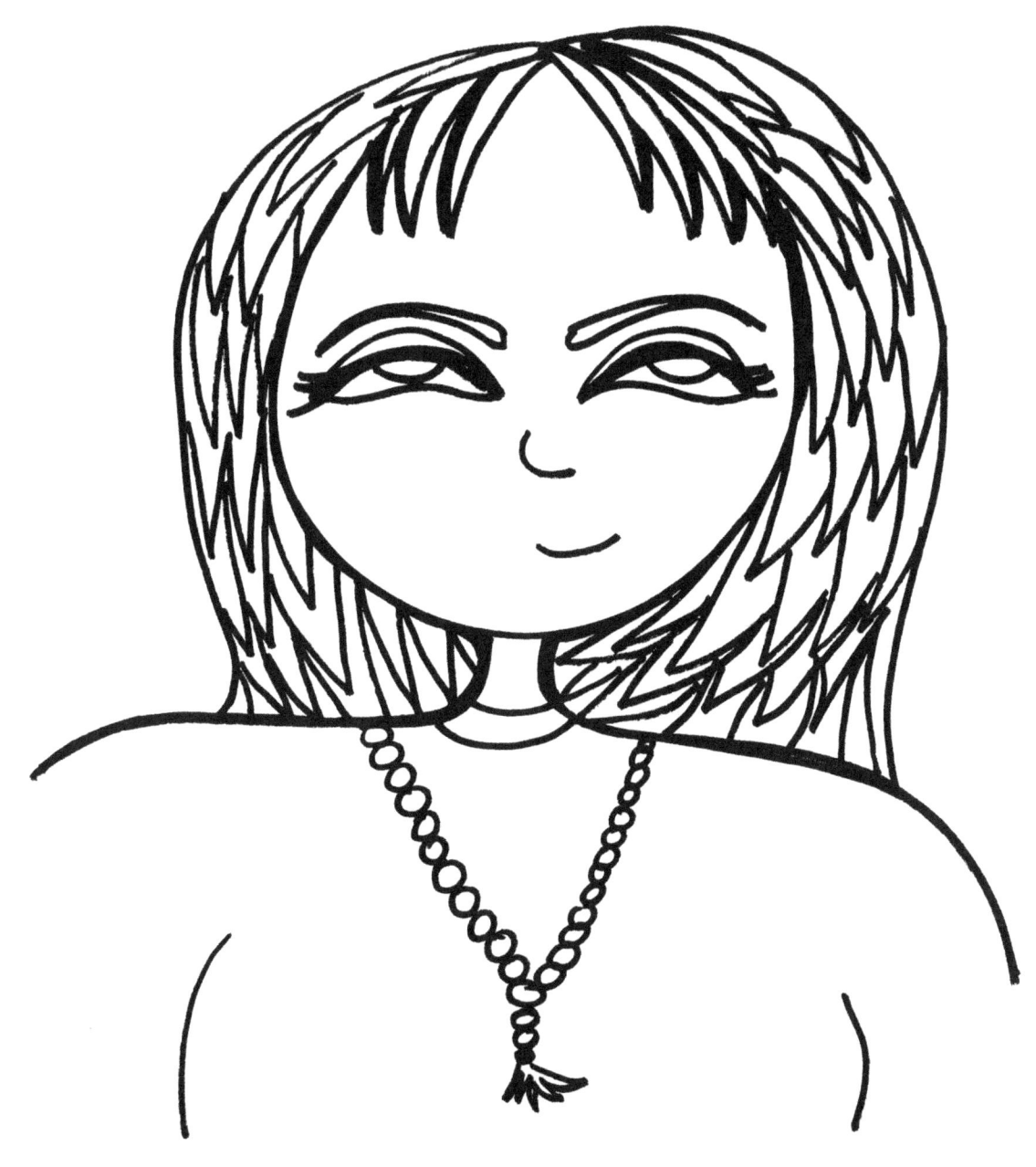

OM Shanti Shanti Shanti

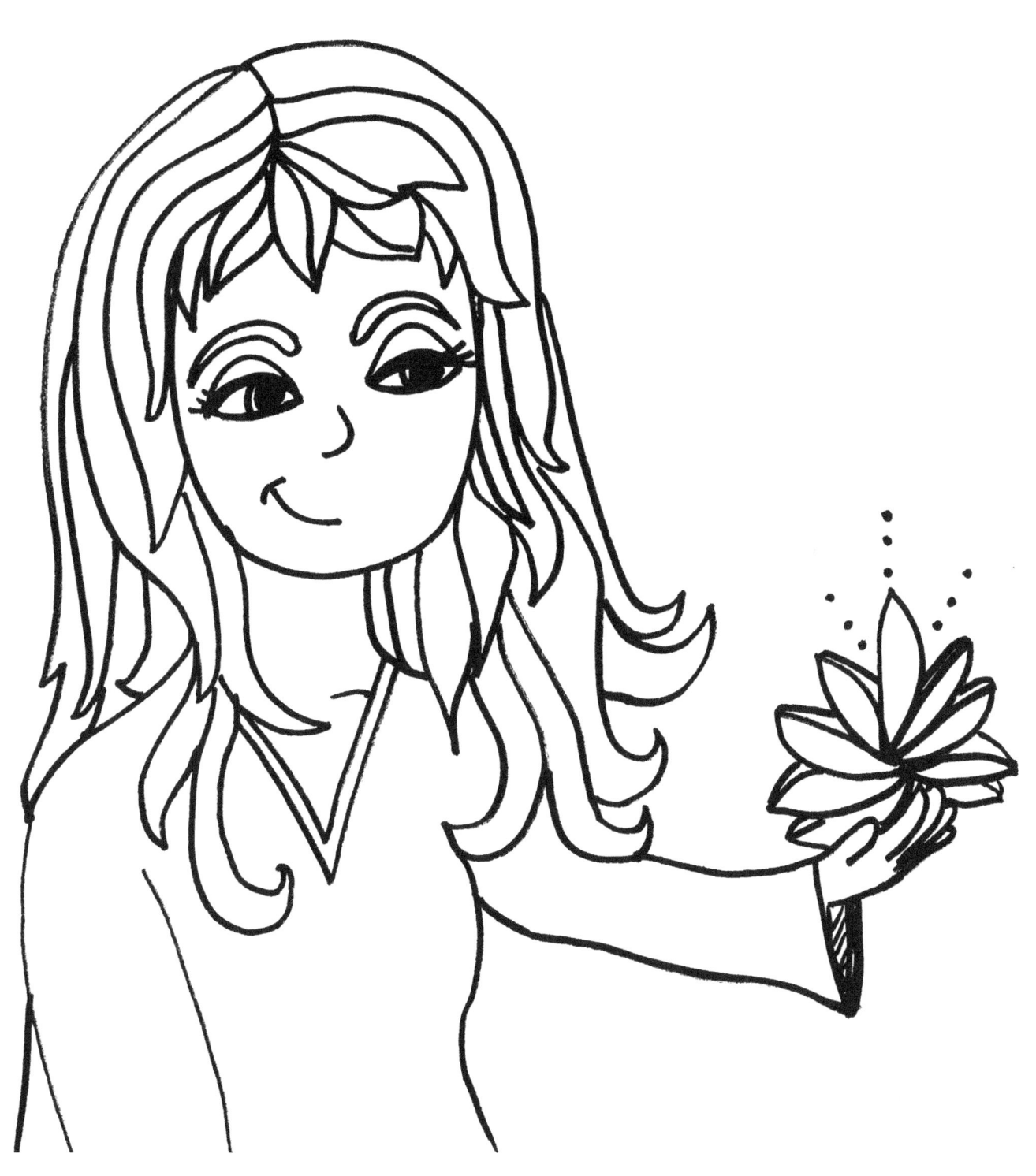

Sat Nam

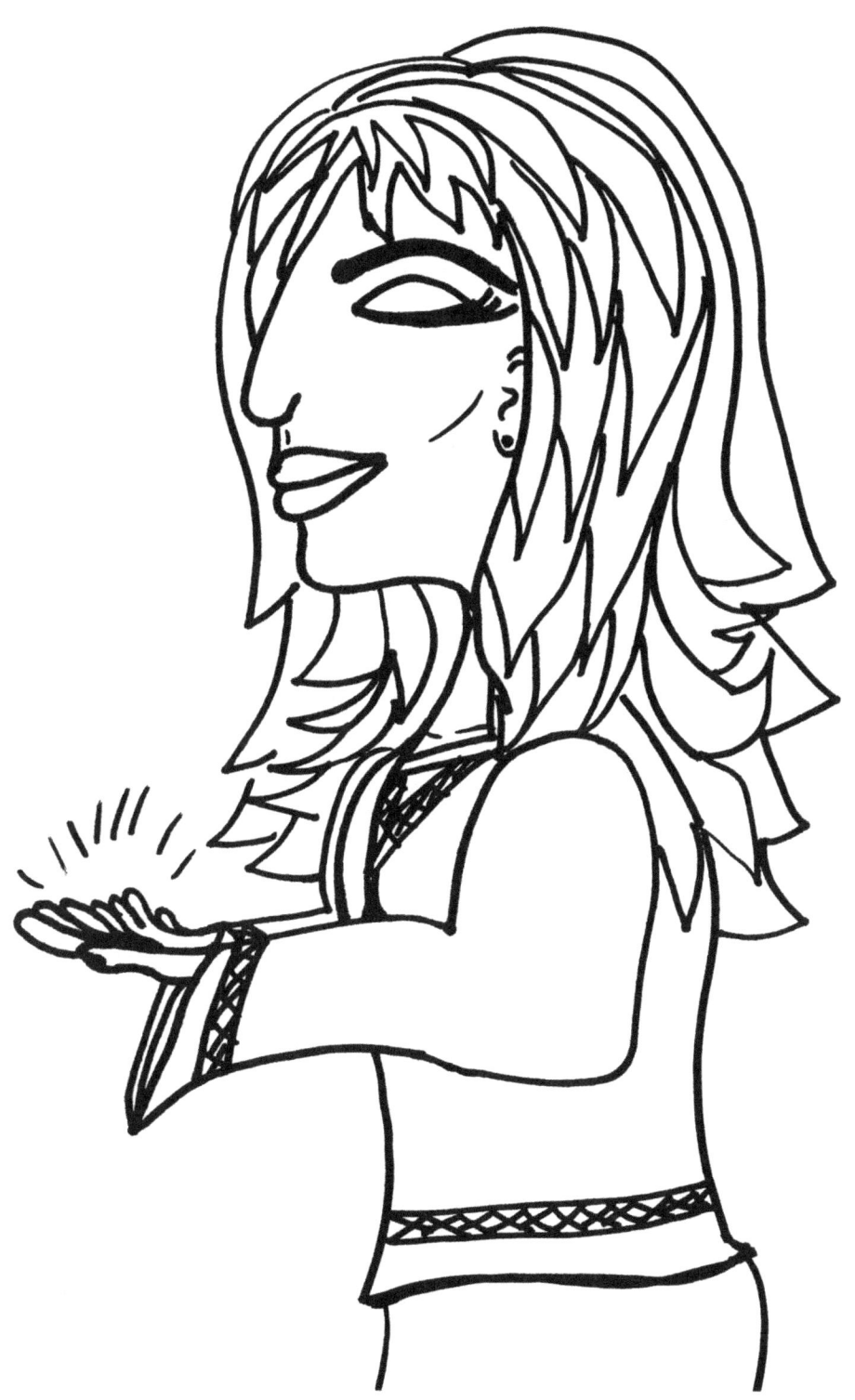

Neti Neti
Not this
Not that

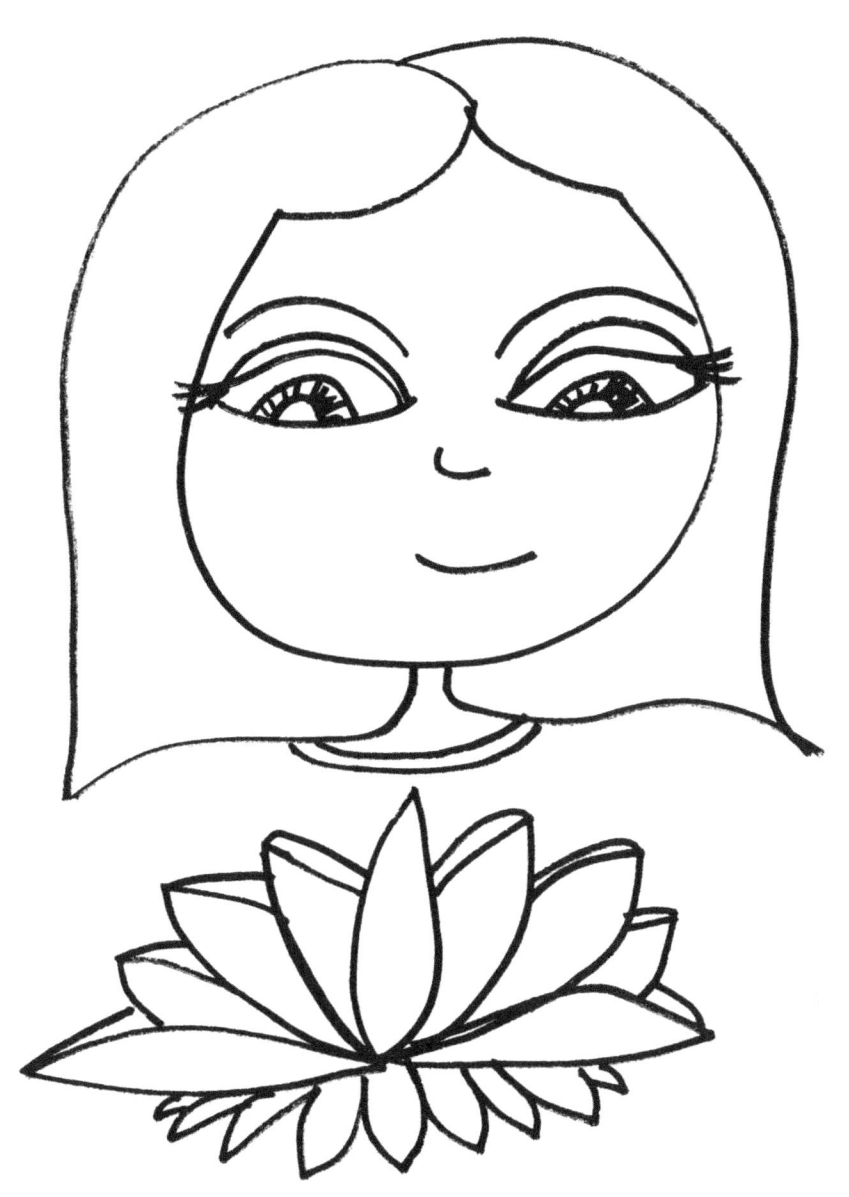

Siri Gaitri Mantra
Ra Ma Da Sa Sa Say So Hung

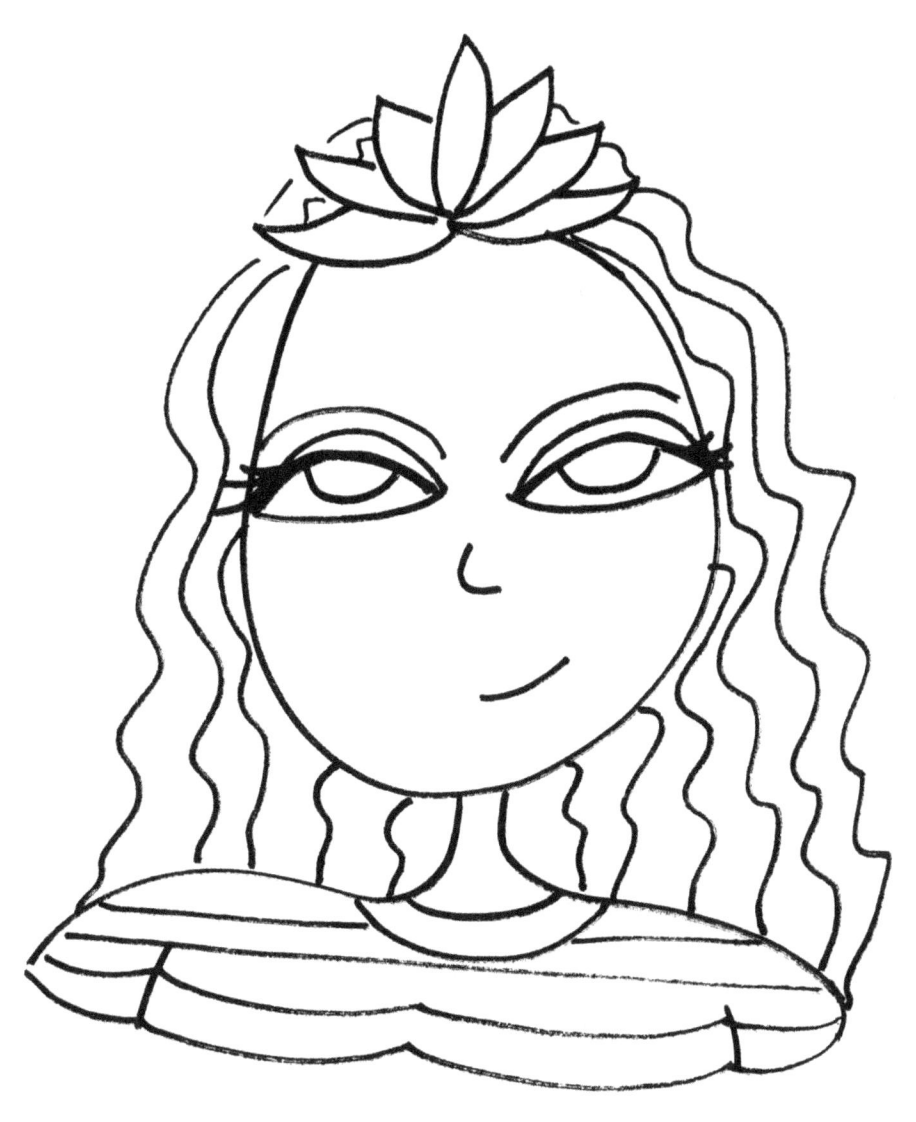

So Hum

Sa ta na ma

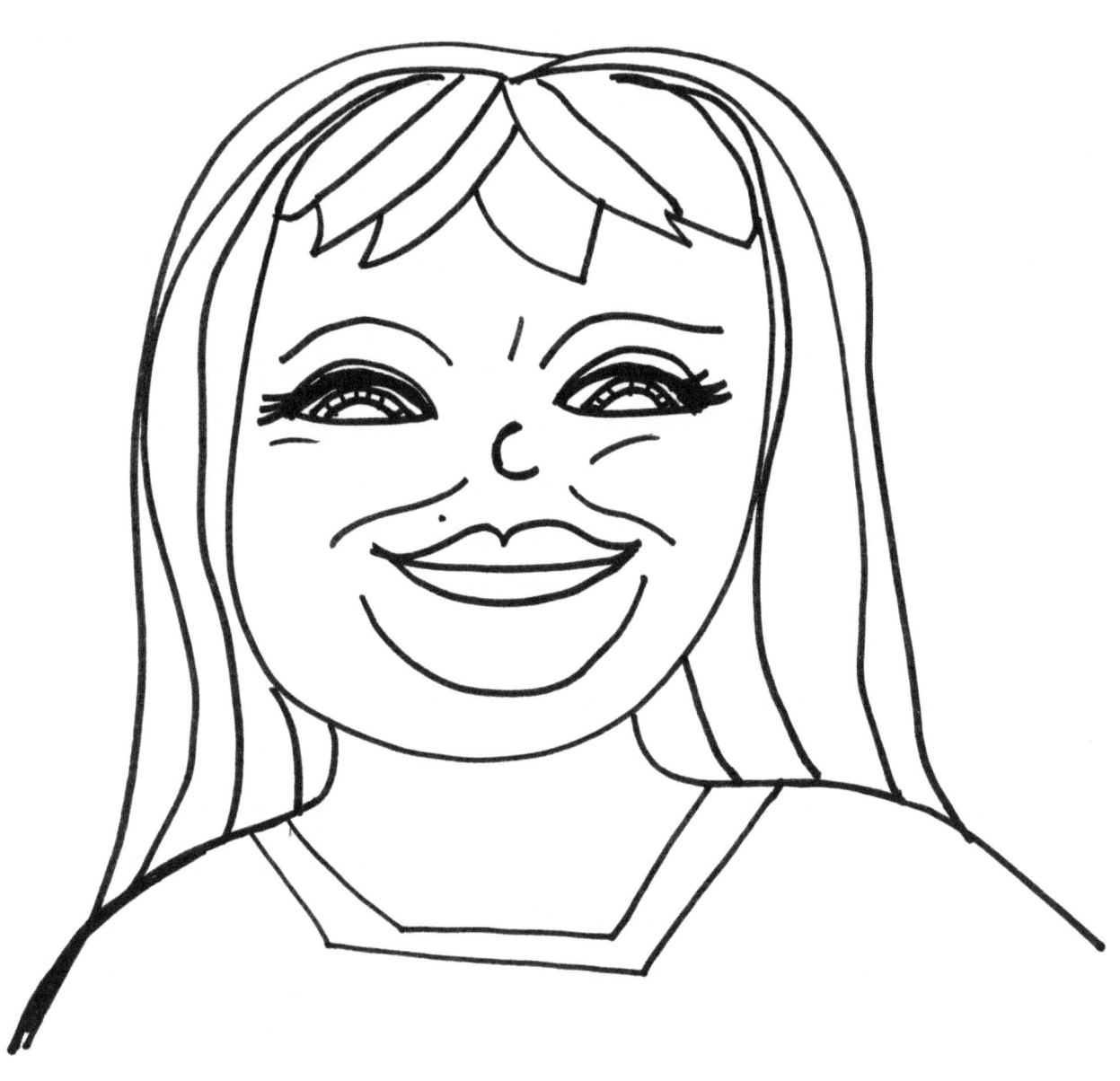

Wahe Guru

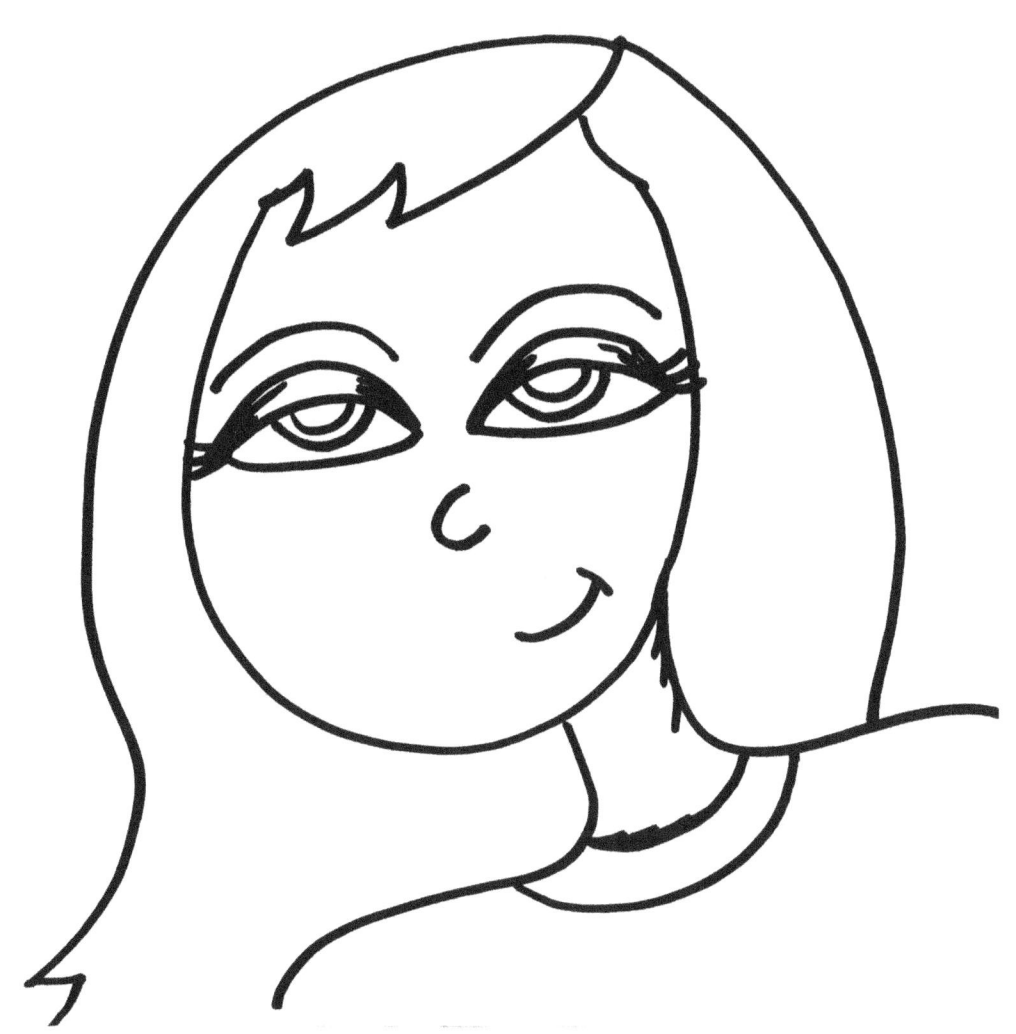

ONG

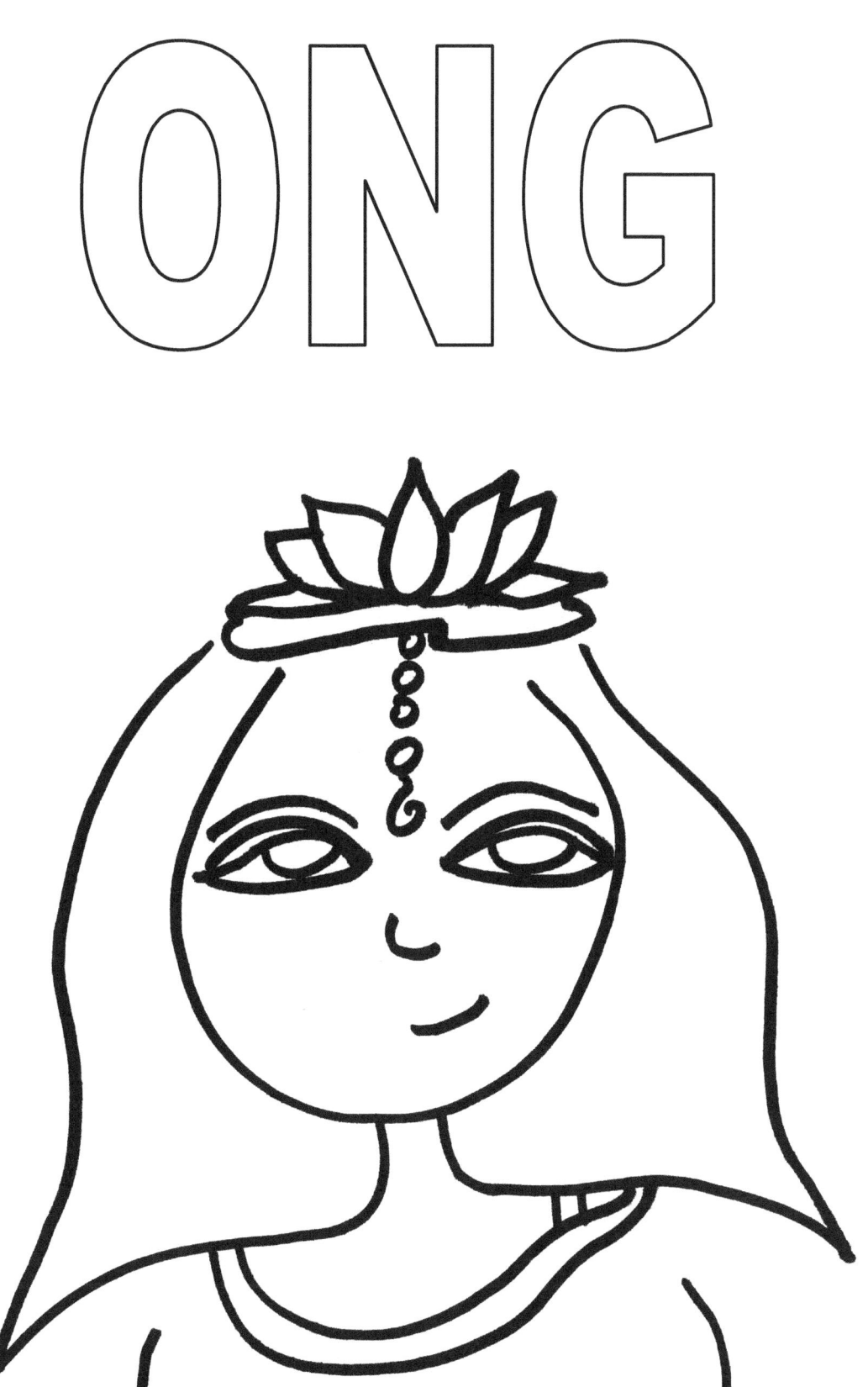

Yam

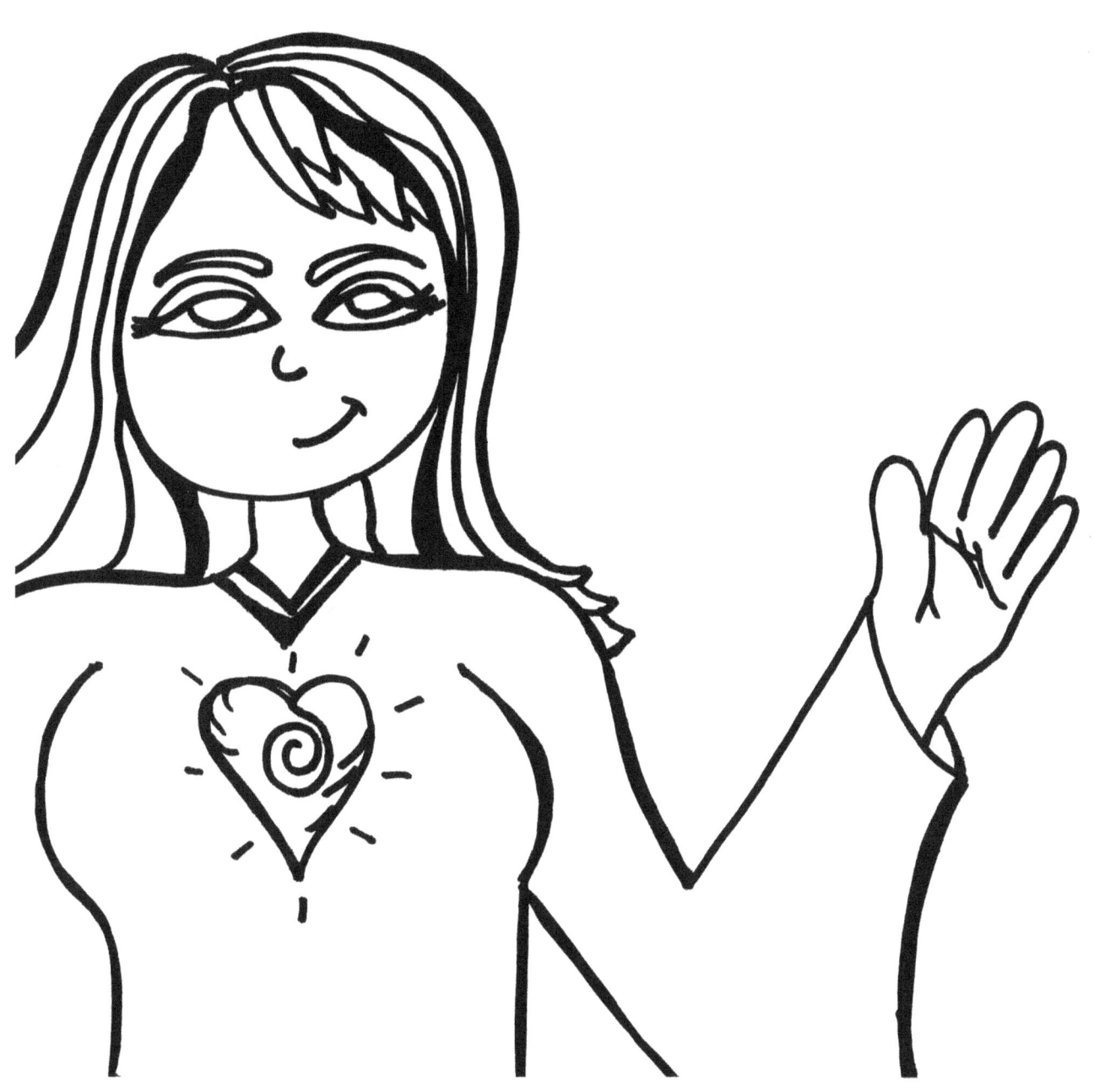

Lam

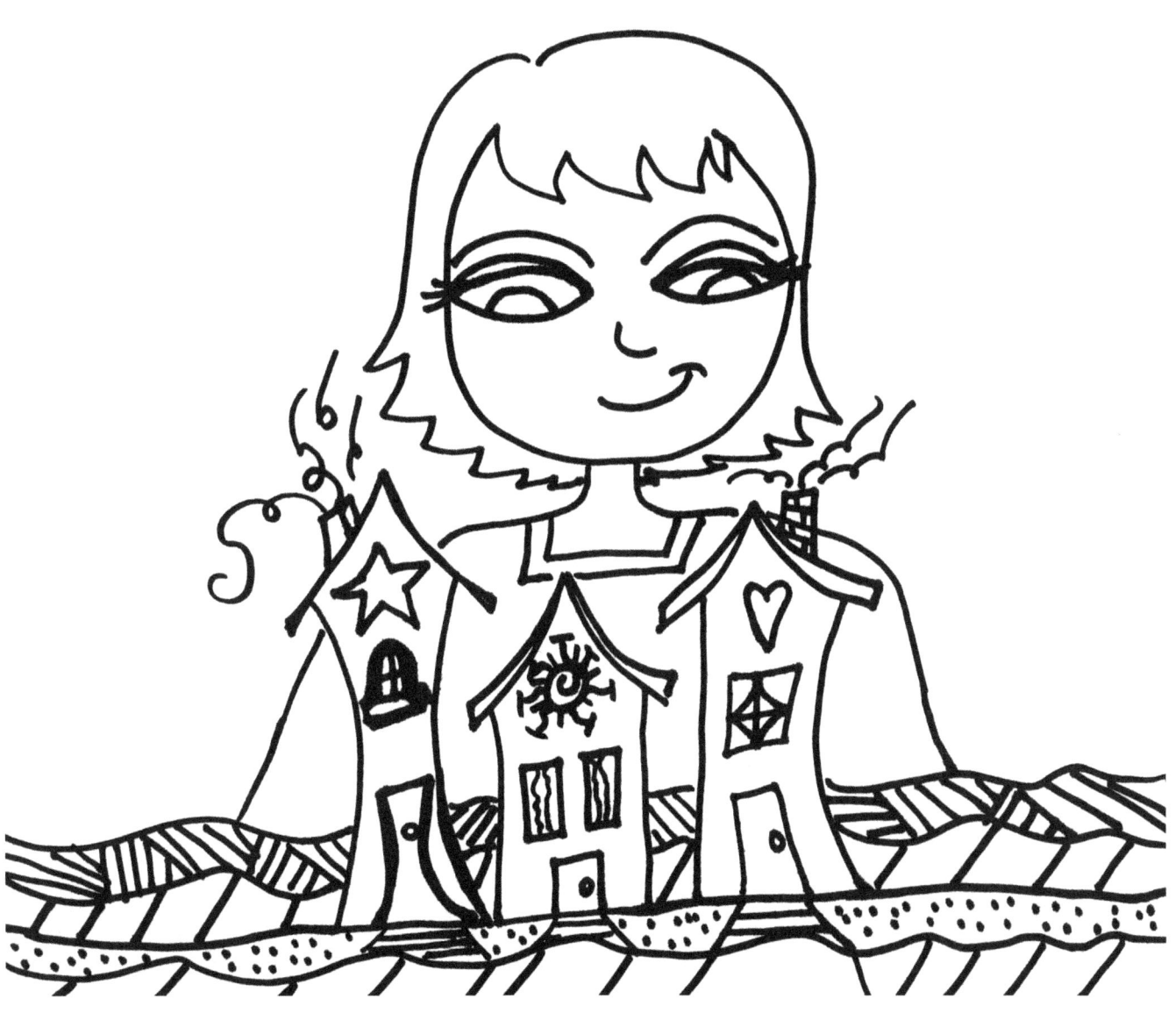

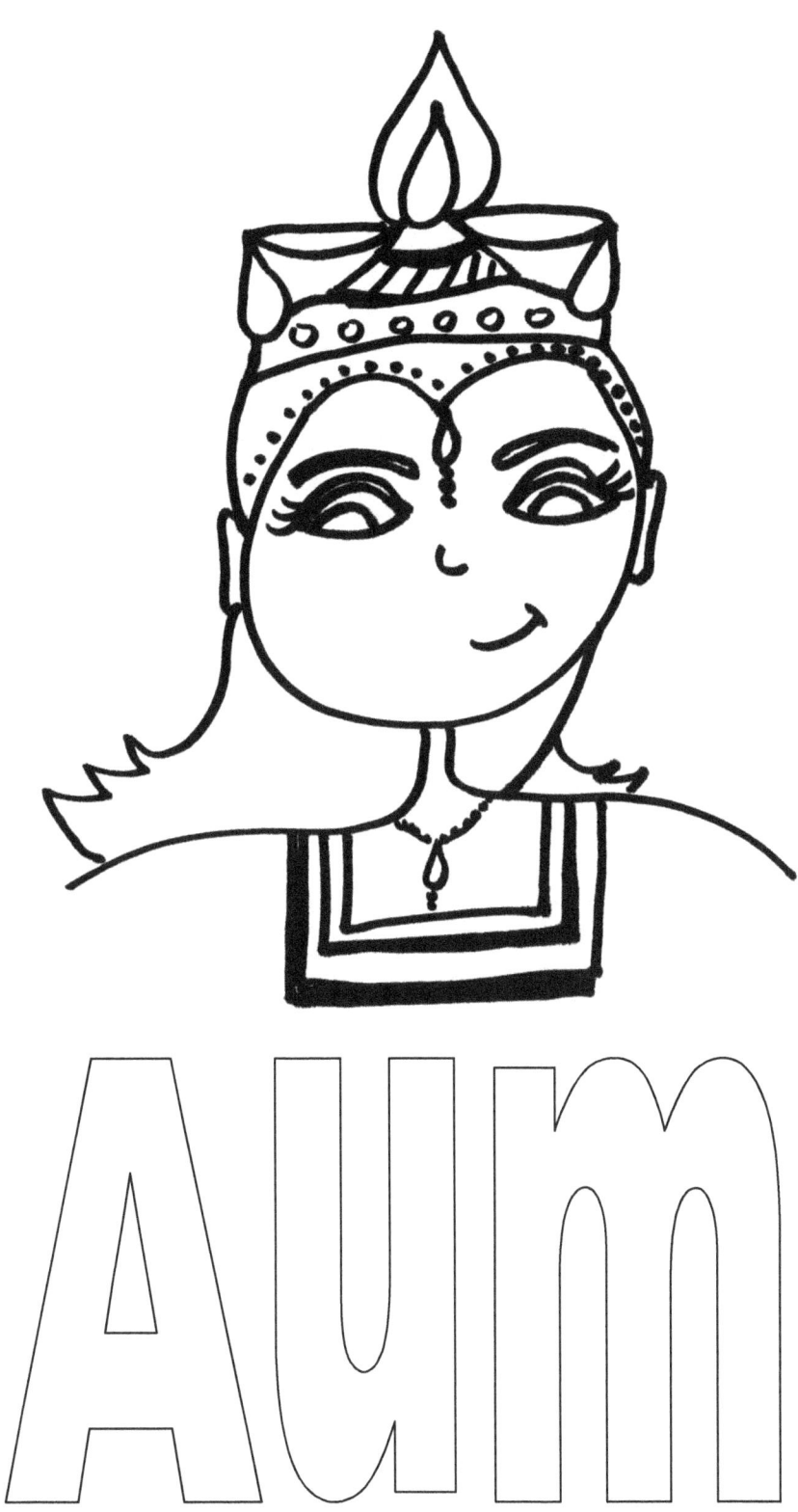

Vam

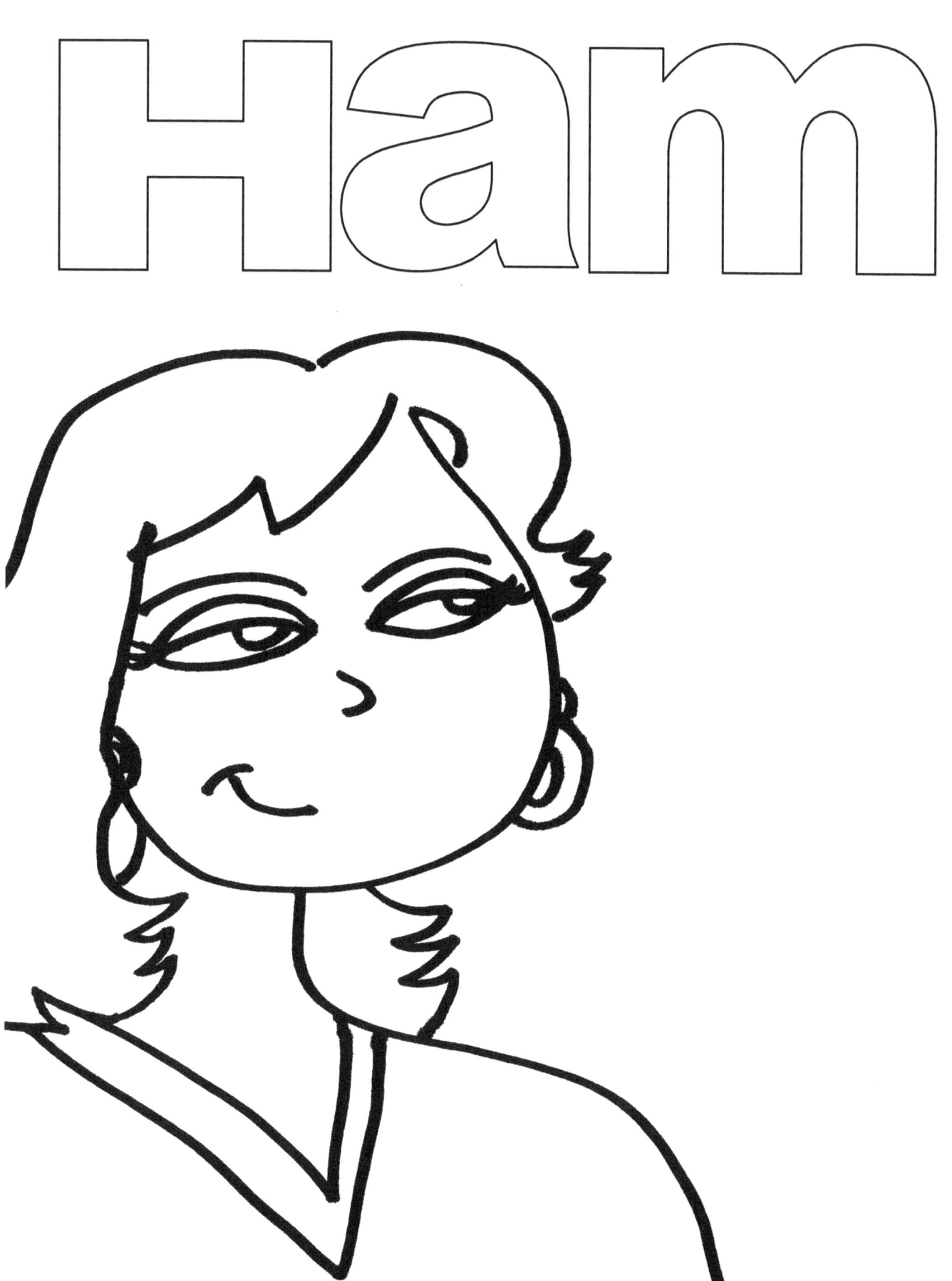

Ham Sah

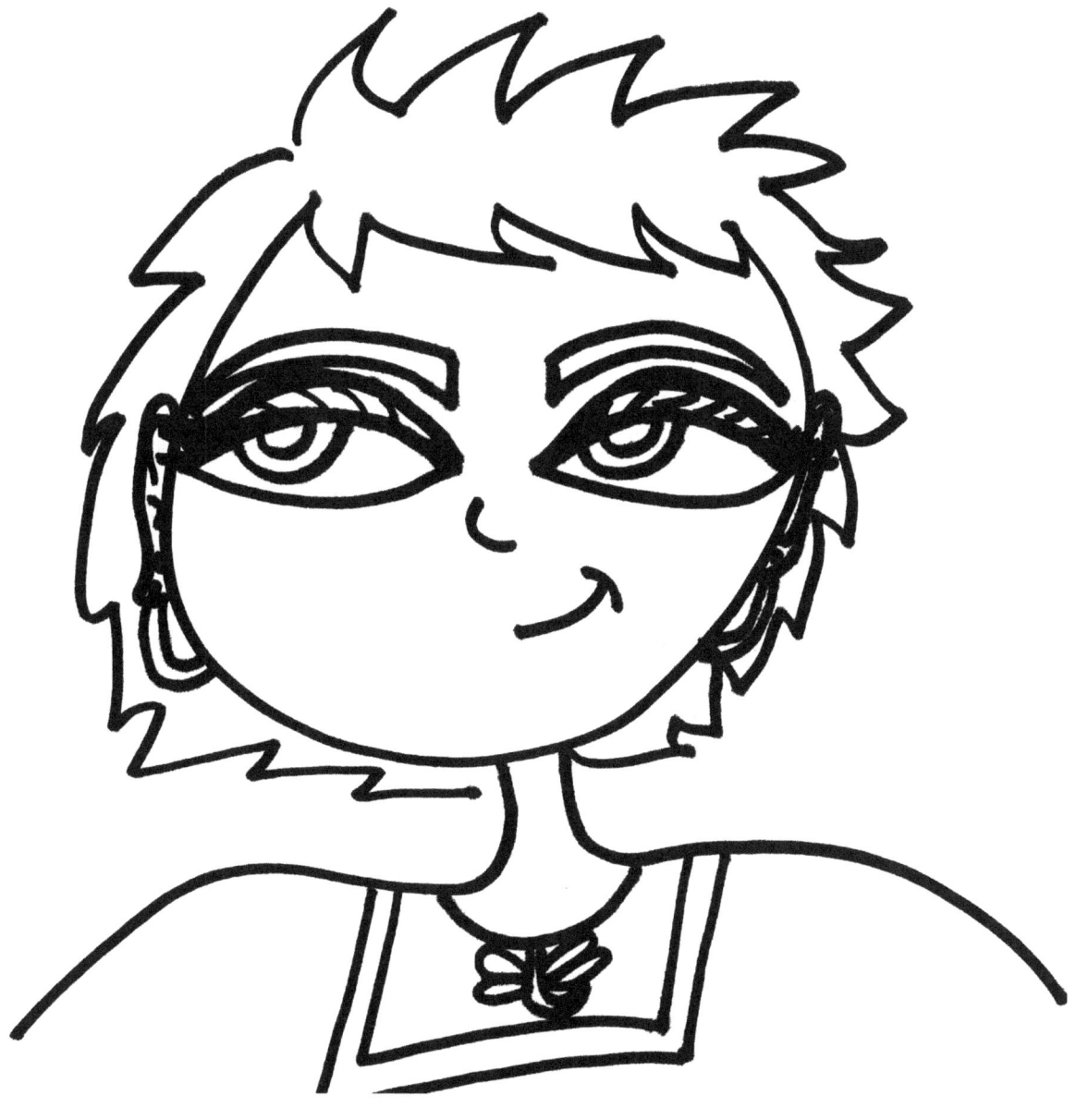

I love you
im sorry
please forgive me
Thank you

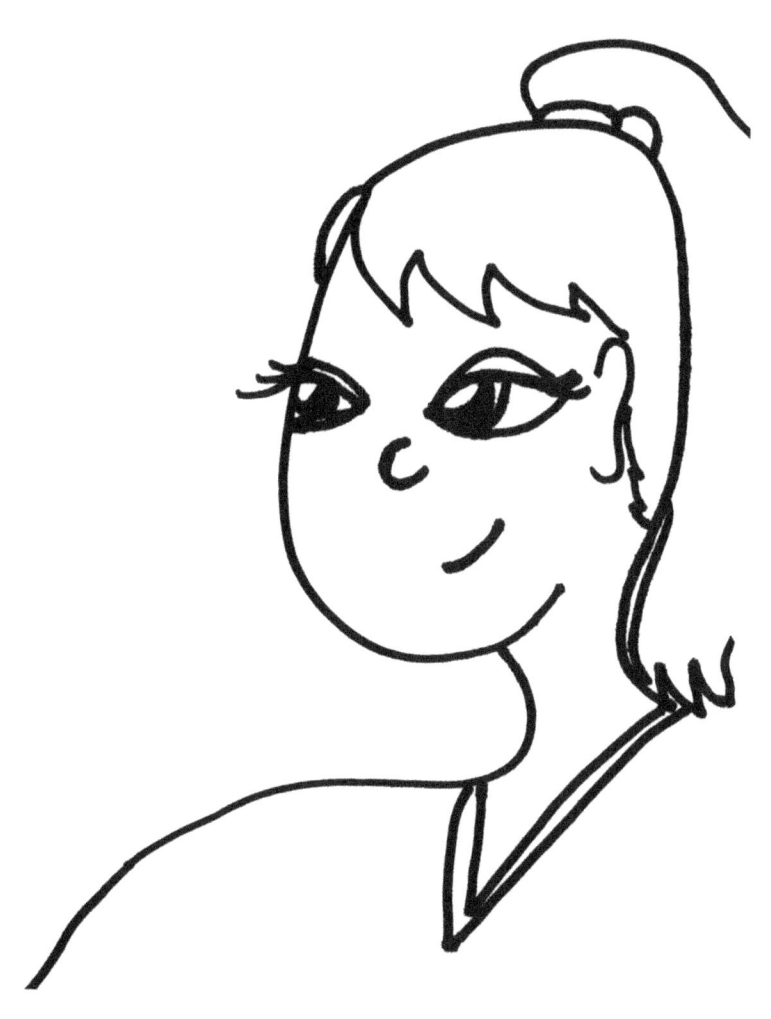

Sat Chit Ananda

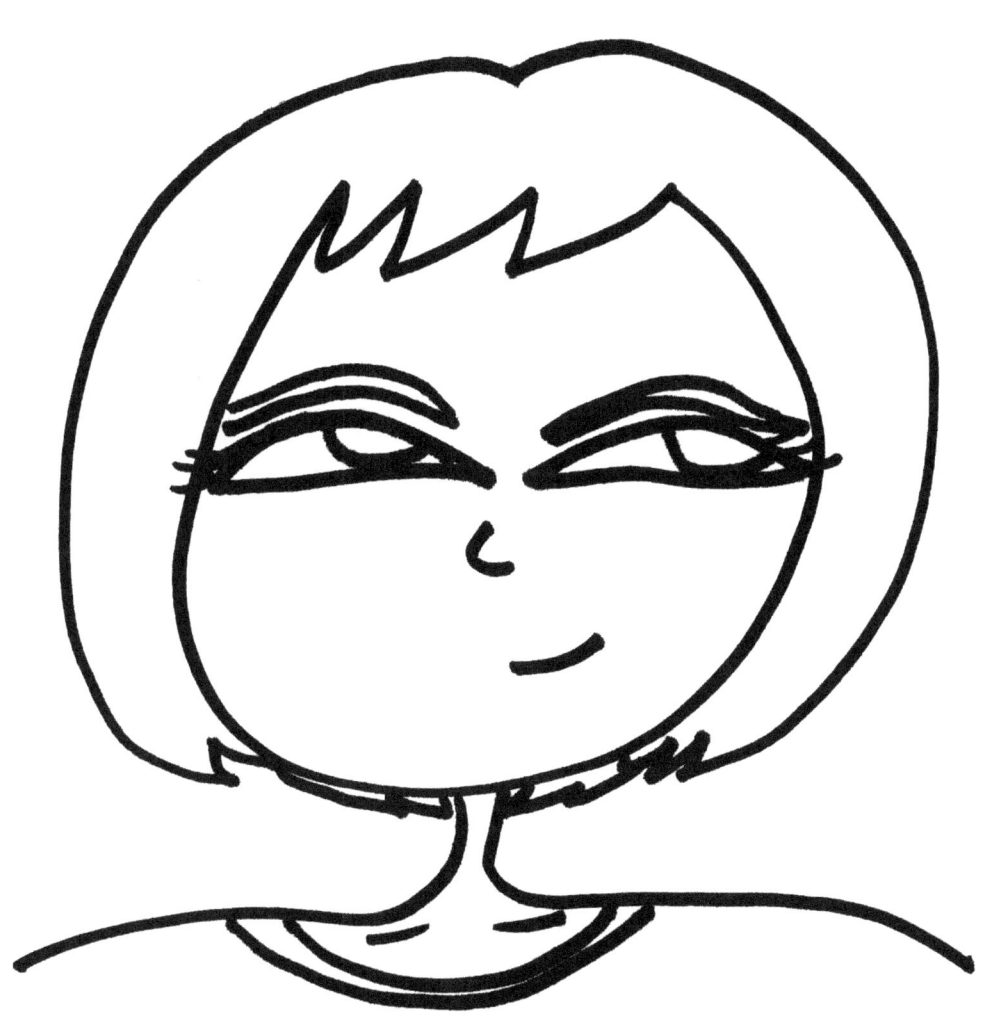

KSham

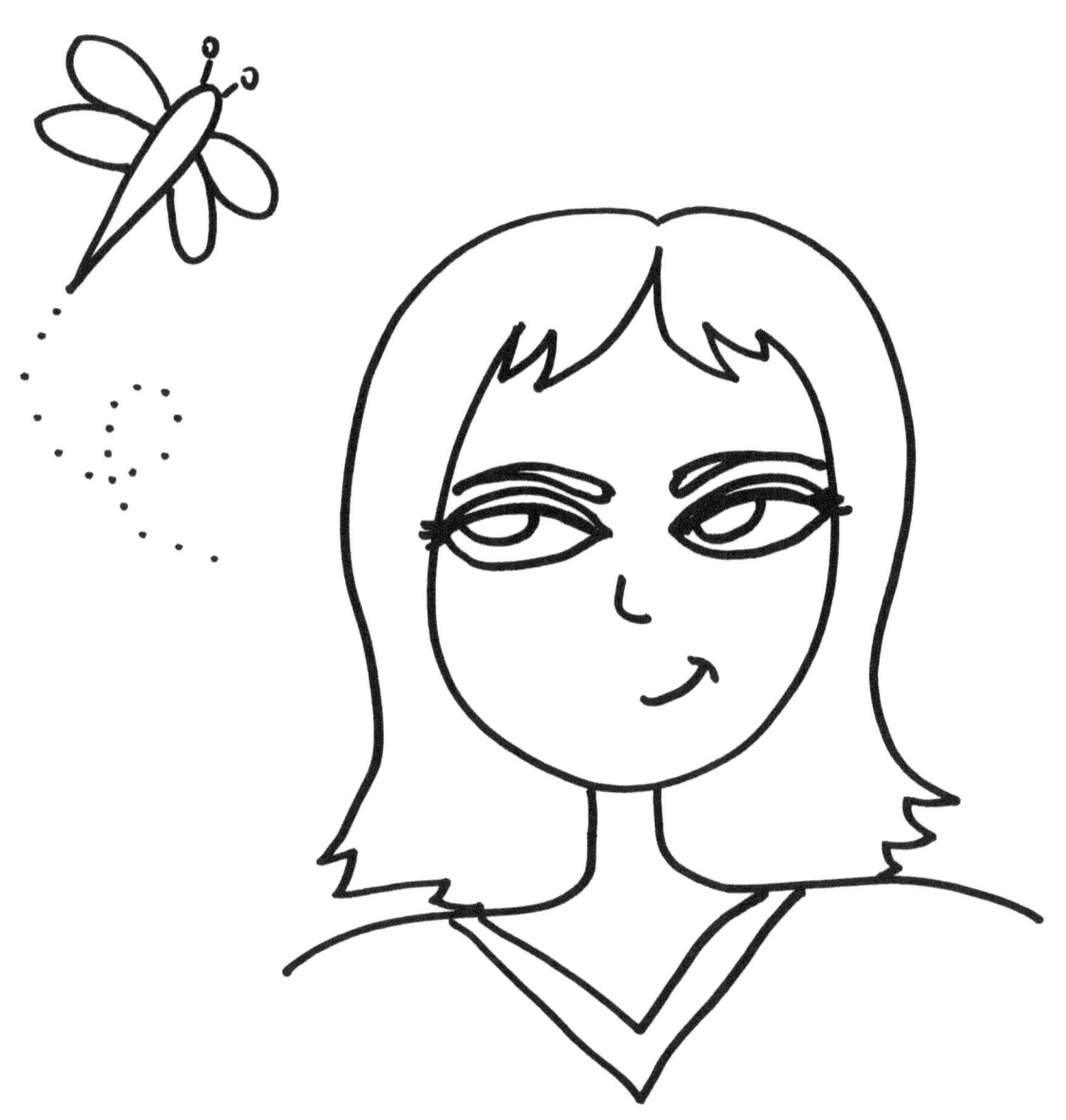

shree ram jay jay ram

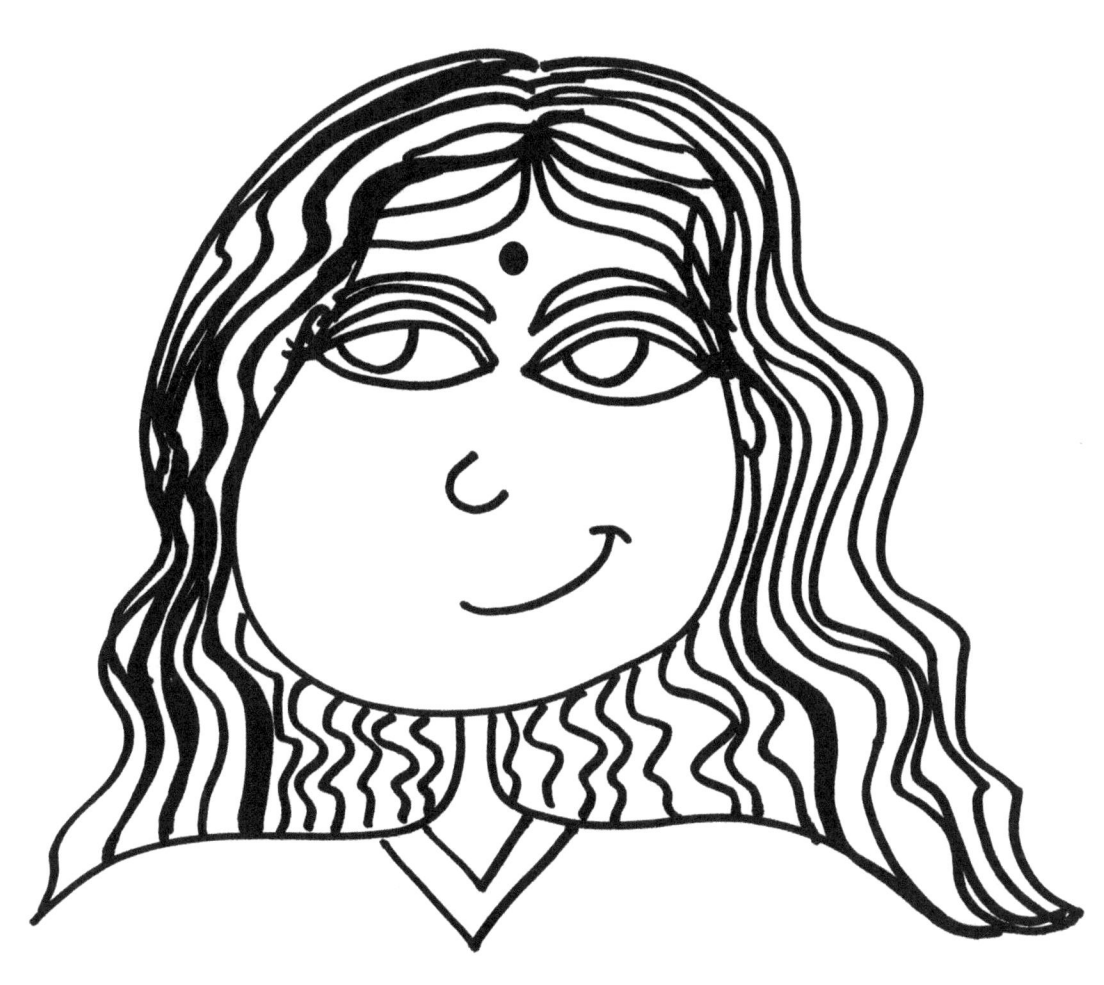

About the Creator:

Tammy Lawrence-Cymbalisty is an Alternative Care provider working in the Kitchener/Waterloo Region. Since 2001 she has helped many people find peace, happiness, harmony and further purpose in their lives.

Tammy holds many degrees including: B.A. Sociology

(Trent University), Certified Yoga Teacher, Reiki

Master/Teacher, HypnoBirthing® Practitioner, Meditation Teacher, Workshop facilitator, Writer, Personal Growth Coach.

She lives with her husband, two felines and a school of fins in Cambridge, ON

Find out more by following Tammy on social media:

http://www.twitter.com/tllc

http://www.tinyurl.com/tlcservices

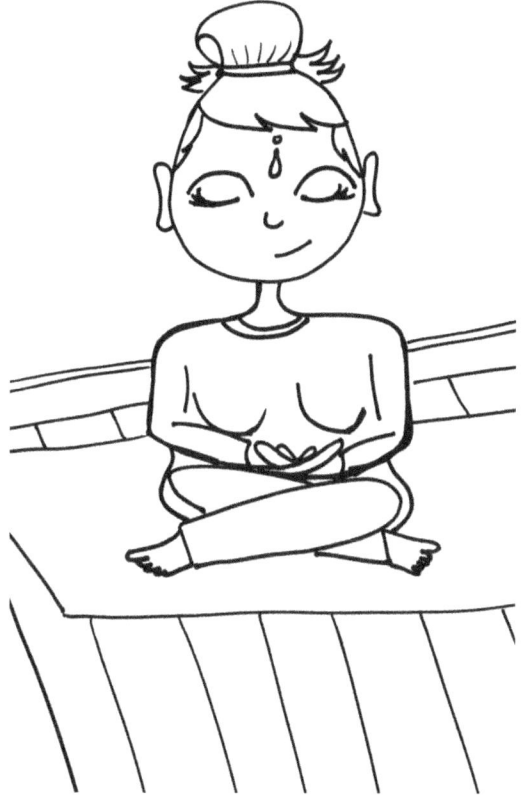

May you find peace

May you find happiness

May you be free from suffering

Namaste, Tammy